This page is intentionally left blank.

Copyright

Intro

Are you bright enough to bring in cash online with Google?

Are you even interested in recognizing how to earn online! Maybe you'll be if you know that a few individuals bring in great money online with Google and Clickbank and furthermore they do it from home. But there are a lot more who fail miserably. All the same it's not precisely about being bright it's more about mental attitude.

The chief factor that differentiates those who discover how to earn online – the achievers – from the losers is that the achievers are geared up to work at it. They don't trust the get rich quick hype, they simply continue building on their small successes till they look around and discover they've learned how to earn online in big quantities and, they have a little empire in the making. Do you believe they're smiling?

This guide will set you on the correct road.

How To Do Keyword Research

There are lots of tools and techniques that can be used to find great keywords. Keywords that will blast your competition out of the water. Here we will look at one strategy.

Choosing Your Techniques

Google Keyword Tool

We all have an astonishing gratis tool at our disposal which instantaneously shows us demand. It's known as the Google Keyword Tool.

To utilize this tool, merely enter a word or phrase, and click on the search button. The Google Keyword Tool will then exhibit you the term you introduced, along with a lot of other related terms. Google may effectively demonstrate demand as they put out the Global Monthly searches for the various terms in the Google search engine.

Utilizing the Keyword Tool to get keyword ideas.

You are able to search for keyword themes by entering a keyword related to your line of work or service or a URL to a page bearing material related to your line of work or service. Or, you are able to go directly to filtering keyword categories next to the will blast your competition out of the water. Here we will look at one strategy.

Choosing Your Techniques

Google Keyword Tool

We all have an astonishing gratis tool at our disposal which instantaneously shows us demand. It's known as the Google Keyword Tool.

To utilize this tool, merely enter a word or phrase, and click on the search button. The Google Keyword Tool will then exhibit you the term you introduced, along with a lot of other related terms. Google may effectively demonstrate demand as they put out the Global Monthly searches for the various terms in the Google search engine.

Utilizing the Keyword Tool to get keyword ideas.

You are able to search for keyword themes by entering a keyword related to your line of work or service or a URL to a page bearing material related to your line of work or service. Or, you are able to go directly to filtering keyword categories next to the statistics table. You are able to utilize one or the other or both collectively; the tool is entirely flexible depending upon how you would like to utilize it. Things to attempt:

Click on Advanced options to additionally fine-tune your search, for instance, by area, language, or mobile search.

Relevant classes will come out to the left. All the same, you are able to click on Show all categories to look at all the categories you can use. Your relevant categories stay highlighted. Choose or deselect the keyword match type checkboxes below the useable categories to further fine-tune your search in the main web browser pane.

Click on the Columns button above the resultants table to custom-make the columns you see inside your results information.

Further keyword ideas utilizing categories or related terms.

After you initially submit keywords or a URL to the Keyword Tool, further keyword sets will come up beneath the useable keyword categories. They'll include common keyword sets that bear the original keyword, in addition to terms that contain both synonyms and terms related to your keyword or URL lookup.

Further keyword sets will come up at a lower place the keyword categories after you've submitted a search utilizing keywords or a site URL.

If you submit simply words or phrases for your search, standard keyword sets that bear the original keyword you put in appear here. For instance, you might put in the word "watches." Your keyword group resultants include keyword sets that contain the term "watches." This might include the keyword set "ladies watches" and "gentlemen's watches." These terms both bear your input keyword.

Further Terms

If you put in both words or phrases and a site URL for your search, further keyword sets might come up. These are all potential terms that bear all of your keywords in any order, including synonyms. They might likewise include terms that are associated if you have submitted a site URL. For instance, if you put in the term "ladies hats," one other word may be "beach hat," which doesn't contain your precise keywords but which is related to ladies hats.

This tool includes the following advantages:

• Discover the most relevant search information from the original Keyword Tool and the Search-based Keyword Tool.
• Look for keyword ideas utilizing any combination of keywords, a URL, and categories.
• Keep particular keyword ideas while you look for fresh ones, by placing stars on your results.
• Download picked out or starred keywords, all keyword outcomes, or all keywords for particular queries.
• Opt to see statistics for Mobile Search, and filter out your results by lookup volume (Global Monthly Searches, and so forth.) and competitor types.
• Equate statistics for your keywords with one or more match sorts at the same time.

Gauging Competition

Have you ever attempted to optimize your internet site for Google and other search engines, only to be unsuccessful at accomplishing the desired outcome you were after? The majority of online marketers sooner or later discover themselves to be rather frustrated with their short comings of search engine success.

Several will simply choose to give up and engage in other methods of traffic. Sadly, this is much of the time an error on their part. The majority of online marketers fail to understand that merely one uncomplicated alteration to their approach to search engine optimization could dramatically improve his or her outcome.

You may be asking, "What is that one uncomplicated alteration? Simple - The answer is keywords. Online traffic success hinges on the keywords you select, and the majority of marketers choose the incorrect ones, which inescapably steers you towards failure and wasted time.

Importance of Keyword Research

Luckily, selecting the correct keywords is a rather elementary and straightforward process. You are not required to be a search engine optimization master, and you are not required to expend a great deal of time, funds, or effort.

In this content I will demonstrate to you how to choose the correct keywords to receive the best possible organic search engine rankings, thereby insuring a costless stream of highly targeted traffic to your internet site.

Prior to beginning with keyword research, we will answer the question: how come search engine traffic is so important for internet site possessors?

Here are some of the key reasons:

• Search engines put together are one of the most immense traffic generators around the world.
• Search engine traffic is composed of extremely targeted traffic.
• Organic search engine traffic is costless.

Furthermore, organic search engine traffic requires very little up keeping and produces small amounts of headaches. When you've gained lead rankings for your "Cash words" (we will specify this term later on), your rankings, oftentimes, will continue for great periods of time. This implies that you aren't required to continuously stress over falling behind on your rankings, thereby allowing you to aim more positive energy towards additional prospects of your business.

As well, holding top rankings in Google (and additional search engines) is a beneficial situation for both you and the search engines.

This is why:

• Google would like to provide people with the most relevant search results possible. Google succeeds when it can supply prime, relevant search results.

• Those who explore on Google succeed when they discover internet sites that yield to them the info they're looking for.

• You succeed by targeting the correct keywords and delivering your web site to the top of the organic search results, therefore gaining the attention of those who are searching for the very subject or niche you are marketing.

So in the end, everybody acquires what they desire. What could be better? With that stated, let's move into the "heart and soul" of keyword searching and how you are able to utilize it to direct clouds of costless search engine traffic to your internet site.

First of all - what is keyword research precisely?

Simply put, keyword research is the substructure of online marketing. If you have knowledge of what phrases or terms your purchasers use to discover data in search engines, you will recognize how to grasp them. You will see precisely which keyword phrases you should concentrate on so that your marketing attempts harvest the most payoffs.

I am certain you have heard the famous marketing tenet, "discover what people desire, then provide it to them." The trouble is, nobody genuinely explains how to execute this. That is where keyword research comes in. It allows you to determine what people genuinely desire.

By being aware of precisely what keywords people are utilizing to search, and by understanding how to pin point those keyword phrases and terms, you will be able to rank at the top of Google's organic search results at any time you wish.

Now we will explore a couple of the primary approaches to keyword research.

Do a self examination and ask yourself if you fall under either or both of these categories:
• Targeting the most eminent search volume keywords in your niche
• Targeting only long-tail keywords in your niche

Although both of these techniques are basic, neither of the pair is ideal.

First of all we will take a look at high search volume keywords.

These oftentimes are keywords that are merely a few words in length, such as "Pink Roses," or simply the term "Flowers." Yes, it perhaps might be a profit generating market, but becoming ranked for such short keywords can be quite complicated.

The amount of additional web sites targeting or contending with you for these keywords is frequently tremendous, so even if you do pull through to the top of the organic results for these keywords, somebody is constantly biting at your heels, attempting to remove you from Google's top page.

It is a non winning situation. You will constantly be contending for the top pages, constantly marketing to remain in the top rankings where others may discover you.

Long-tail keyword targeting as well bear severe drawbacks.

These are terms, words, or long phrases consisting of between four, five, or more words inside any granted keyword phrase. (For example, "pink flowers mature best in organic soil".)

The trouble with long-tail keywords is that they capture small amounts traffic if any from month to month. You are recommended to target and keep up high-ranking results for hundreds, if not thousands, of keywords to bring forth adequate traffic to continuously maintain a profit generating internet site. That is a great deal of hard work. Producing material for that many keywords is time depleting and may be very pricey.

That leads us to a master of techniques for executing keyword research - targeting "Cash words." This approach analyzes keywords in a more scientific manner.
A "Cash word" is a keyword that consists of really high search volume (high numbers of people are searching for the keyword from month to month) and really low competition in the search engines (small amounts of internet sites are targeting the keyword).

The profits of targeting Cash words are plenty:

• You will accomplish multiple first-page ranking in Google's organic results in the matter of weeks, and occasionally even within days.
• You will spend minimal effort.
• Your site ranking will adhere to the top of the organic search results like crazy glue.

All of this leads to long-term, automated traffic.

Gauging The Advertising Demand For A Cickbank Keyword

In a previous chapter I discussed the importance of distinguishing and targeting search keywords that are not excessively competitive, but bear potential to bring in enough searches to construct a money making web site around.

The Competition

We will now go step by step through the process of discovering these "Cash words."

It is recommended to discover keywords bringing in an excess of 500 searches on a monthly basis. At the same time you want to have less than 10,000 competing pages for that specific keyword. The greater the search volume on a monthly basis and the fewer the competitors, the more profitable the keyword.

You are able to punch any keyword you choose in and immediately determine whether it's poor, fair, good, excellent, or a money maker. Let's discuss a real life example of how to apply this, so that you are able to implement it to your own niche.

To start out, you will want to type the general niche subject into Google's External Keyword Tool.

For instance, if you type the term "Flowers" into Google's external keyword tool, you will receive hundreds of results. These results are the terms related to flowers others are in reality searching with as they are searching for information.

You will discover three different settings you should use for your beginning keyword research:
Spell out the niche topic into the search area.

Adjust your Match Type to "phrase." Do not give an excessive amount of detail, this yields more precise data to base your keyword research on. Some individuals use the precise term, and that is an outstanding piece of advice for PPC advertising. But for info on organic search results, I would rather use the phrase match. (The "precise" match is excessively restrictive).

Utilize the advanced filter to get rid of any keywords or keyword phrases that acquire less than 500 worldwide searches on a monthly basis from the results.

We're utilizing the United States as the locale. Utilizing another nation, even if you reside in that nation, isn't going to provide you with the entire possible audience, since you are marketing to individuals all around the world.

However, the amount of contending pages for that specific term is over 6 million - which signifies over 6 million other individuals are competing for it.

How exactly did I find the amount of competing pages?

Go to Google's home site and type the term inside quotes. It is crucial that you use the quotes because they ensure that you acquire the correct phrase match search results well as the proper amount of competing pages. Among the terms that arose in our example above was "Flower Drawings," which obtains over 6 thousand worldwide searches on a monthly basis.

Once we placed this phrase into Google's search engine within quotes, the number of possible competing pages is over 12 thousand. Realize where this is going?

We have discovered a Cash word!

This is an example of an excellent keyword phrase to construct a page on your web site about. You may choose to have pencil drawings, or possibly post an article on drawing methods to produce the best flower drawings. This type of web page or article has great potential to be ranked at the top of the organic search results in as little as days or weeks, and can direct continuous traffic to your website.

Discovering a dozen or so of these types of Cash word keywords will weld your website, articles, and material at the top of Google's organic search results and direct numerous visitors to your website each and every month.

You unquestionably want to hold on to all the good keywords, but do not toss out all those "Fair" keywords quite yet. They may be of value in discovering additional Cash words.

First, however, I would like to tell you that very few individuals are going to commit the time to do manual research for keywords in this fashion.

This implies that if you are willing to take the time to do your due diligence, you are going to be far ahead of the game when it concerns competing for search engine rankings.

Using Wordtracker

Wordtracker will assist you in writing client-centered and search-engine-friendly internet site copy. Whether you sell merchandise or publish info online, you can't do without the mighty insights that keyword research will provide you.

A Tool You Should Know

Wordtracker can:

• Aim traffic to your web site by utilizing the words individuals utilize when they're searching.

• Compose awesome site copy by integrating terms that individuals instantly identify with.

• Design profitable PPC campaigns by building a full range of keyword phrases that will captivate your market.

• Formulate awesome content themes that directly address your clients' needs.

• Comprehend your buyers' behavior and interests by analyzing the words that they utilize.

• Appraise the size of a potential net market by the number of searches carried on, and

• Formulate fresh revenue streams by utilizing popular keywords to prompt fresh product and service themes.

Using Wordtracker

A vital opening move of search-engine optimization (SEO) is choosing great keywords for your site. Many individuals go on the net and look for a keyword through a search engine like Google.

As the internet has evolved to buyer- centered searching, keyword selection and SEO have gotten to be key tasks in building site traffic and a solid net presence. Wordtracker provides a tool that makes the keyword-selection procedure easy.

Initially, brainstorm a few related keywords for your site. Think about which keywords your target buyers would type into a search engine to discover your products and services. Save up a list of likely keywords to check in Wordtracker.

Sign up at Wordtracker to get access to the free tools. (https://freekeywords.wordtracker.com/users/sign_up.)

Using Wordtracker

A vital opening move of search-engine optimization (SEO) is choosing great keywords for your site. Many individuals go on the net and look for a keyword through a search engine like Google.

As the internet has evolved to buyer- centered searching, keyword selection and SEO have gotten to be key tasks in building site traffic and a solid net presence. Wordtracker provides a tool that makes the keyword-selection procedure easy.

Initially, brainstorm a few related keywords for your site. Think about which keywords your target buyers would type into a search engine to discover your products and services. Save up a list of likely keywords to check in Wordtracker.

Sign up at Wordtracker to get access to the free tools. (https://freekeywords.wordtracker.com/users /sign_up.)

Travel to Wordtracker's free keyword-suggestion tool. Put in a keyword or keyword phrase and submit.

Go over the results, searching for keywords that are looked for a great deal. The greatest keyword searches will be named at the top, along with the list of monthly searches. Center on the most popular, often looked for keywords.

Add keywords to your list that Wordtracker might have suggested that weren't on your list earlier. Now continue digging deeper and deeper and you'll discover keyword phrases that will be extremely centered search terms with less competition than pursuing core keywords.

You will start to find keyword phrases that you can target that you may never have come up with on your own.

Converting Traffic

Each search has an individual behind it.

The words typed into search engines disclose an amazing amount about visitor intention. You need to Understand as much as you are able to about your possible buyers, and utilize keywords that disclose intention to buy your products.

Begin by thinking about your likely buyers' motivations and intention.

What sorts of inquiries will they be making?
What are they attempting to achieve?
Utilize these questions to begin a list of
keywords to research.

2 sorts of customers

A few of your customers will be methodical
and ordered, asking numerous "how" and
"what" questions. How can I write a better
book, how can I be healthier, how can I eat
vegetarian, for example.

Other people are more emotional and
relational in their plan of attack. Spontaneous
and human-centered sorts are concerned with
the experience and the results: best-
performing eBook, healthiest face cream,
broadening life, for example.

How do you think like your customer?

Remember that people don't have to be a
vegetarian to see the advantage of eating
healthier.

Additional questions you are able to ask: how
come they're thinking about going vegetarian?
Is it chiefly wellness? Is it chiefly cultural, love
of beasts, spiritual? Where are they at in the

purchasing procedure for information and products?

Think across-the-board and all-encompassing. Bring your list to Wordtracker Keyword Tool. Utilize it as a beginning point to explore particular terms, and likewise utilize the thesaurus feature. Accumulate a few less specific terms around "vegetarian food", for instance. Make certain that they're particular enough to fit your business.

On the net, traffic will cost you money sometimes, so think select keywords, not quantity. Now you are able to begin adding terms that correspond most closely with your visitors' intention in regard to what you sell.

Prioritize for getting the conversion.

Prioritize the keywords not simply on the sum of traffic potential, but by clear-cut intention. You have to likewise take into account the power of your product to deliver the value that will get this traffic to buy. It's all right to add terms with really tiny traffic potential if they've a high chance of converting.

These are the words you will not only wish to optimize your pages for, but words that you'll wish to be present in your material. If you require a bigger result, then you'll likewise wish to utilize these keywords in your anchor text.

Using Paid Tools Like Market Samurai

Keyword inquiry is the most inherent part of an SEO campaign and it's has to done with complete care. Commonly we utilize the gratis keyword tool available and get a few facts and figures on the keywords. A big number of individuals utilize Google Keyword Tool.

Much of the time we get a few satisfactory keyword reports and use that information for further SEO activities.

This is all right with little sites or sites which have a market that don't have any severe search engine rivalry. However in the case of sites that have ferocious search engine rivalry, the gratis tools might not be adequate. They might not be able to supply keyword information from all the angles.

This is where a paid keyword inquiry tool comes into play.

A Closer Look

A few of the huge benefits of utilizing a paid keyword research tool:

More Elaborate Information
Different than the gratis keyword research tools, the paid tools supply more detailed and broadened information which helps us to analyze the keywords more efficiently.

Multiple Search Engines

Paid keyword research instruments let you to accumulate keyword data from multiple search engines, which helps you to examine your keywords in a brighter way.

More Interactive Content

Many of the paid keyword research tools are capable of supplying more interactive reports like graphs which are much simpler to comprehend.

Efficiency

Keyword inquiry utilizing paid keyword research tools truly saves a lot of time when likened to the free tools. There's lots of advanced characteristics which makes the keyword research procedure faster.

More Dependable

As the keyword research tools get information from multiple sources, you get more reliable information and figures. This helps us in making our keyword research more effective.

Effective for SEM

Instead of benefiting for SEO Keyword research, paid keyword tools likewise help us to acquire more data for our SEM or paid marketing actions, which in turn help us to work out a better marketing budget.

Market Samurai

If you open up Market Samurai you'll discover the accompanying modules:

• Keyword Research – determine extra related keywords for your seed keyword and break down their traffic, Adwords value, rivalry, purchasing intention and more.
• SEO Rivalry – Market Samurai will get a look at the top 10 outcomes for your keyword and demonstrate how well they rank for a number of crucial SEO elements.
• Rank Tracker – Add in your URLs and keywords, and Market Samurai will demonstrate where your web site ranks for every one of your keywords over time on Google, Yahoo and Bing.

• Monetization – discover products to market on Clickbank, Amazon, CJ, and PayDot.
• Discover Material – discover ebooks related to your keywords, which you are able to add to your site or blog.
• Publish Material – oversee all your WordPress blogs in one place and put out your content simply
• Marketing – discover Web 2.0 web sites, blogs and bulletin boards that are related to your keyword where you are able to put your links.

Keyword Research

If constructing niche sites, doing the right keyword research is the key to success. You need to discover keywords that acquire much traffic, but don't have so much rivalry that they're impossible to rank for. To begin with the keyword research module, you initially have to insert a seed keyword.

Push the Generate Keywords button and Market Samurai will travel out to Google and generate a list of relevant keywords to go with your seed keywords. You are able to filter this first list by an assortment of criteria, such as traffic, phrase length, and favorable and negative keywords.

Following, you'll need to drill down into every keyword by pushing the Analyze Keywords button. There is a ton of data it may search for every keyword including traffic stats (SEO and Adwords) and assorted SEO rivalry components. You are able to then filter these analyzed outcomes by adjusting thresholds for any of the different elements to come up with a fistful of awesome keywords to really target.

Keyword Rivalry

When you've discovered a few great prospective keywords, the following step is to examine them with the SEO rivalry module. In here, Market Samurai will get out and view the top ten search resultants for your keyword and show you in a simple to read table how these sites rate for an assortment of long-familiar SEO factors.

These take into account domain age, Google page rank, list of back-links and keyword in title and URL numbers. It's truly nice how Market Samurai utilizes color codes the assorted cells, so you are able to tell at a glance how tough it would be to rank for your keyword. Red means hard, yellow is fair, and green is simple. So if the SEO rivalry table is satiated with red cells, you know immediately that ranking for this keyword will be really ambitious.

Rank Tracker

When you have chosen the perfect keyword, and have assembled a web site around it, you'll soon need to track how well your web site is ranking for that keyword. That is where the Rank Tracker module enters.

Here you are able to insert in a list of domains, and then a number of keywords you wish to track for that domain. Choose the search engines you wish to check and Market Samurai will travel out to every one and tell you where your URL ranks for every keyword in your list.

You'll view the actual page URL on your domain that's ranking, as well as its list of back-links and page rank. The Rank Tracker will likewise keep track of your placement and number of back-links and you are able to extract a nice looking graph to discover how your web site has bettered over time.

Market Samurai works on both Windows and Mac. It's a crazily powerful software for net marketers, and I only touched on the few modules I utilize most. The software is really able to do a great deal more too.

Paid Traffic On Google Versus Free Traffic On Google

Many search engines nowadays have 2 primary sorts of search results: organic results (a.k.a. "natural search outcomes") are search outcomes that are accumulated based on the search engines algorithm, and are commonly influenced by a couple of factors, like the number and caliber of other sites who have decided to link to a result, the age/expertness of the web site.

The 2nd sort of search outcome is called Pay Per Click (PPC) these are advertisements that consist of businesses yielding money to the search engine to come up on top of search results if a particular keyword is searched.

Both natural search optimization (called SEO) and PPC have their benefits and disfavors and it's wise to evaluate every technique on an individual basis to see which of these may render the keenest result for the least price.

Different Choices

Adwords/PPC

Nowadays PPC ads are the basic technique by which many search engines return revenue, for the sake of this discussion I'll center on AdWords, which is Google's PPC system and is the biggest PPC system presently on the net.

PPC has a few clear benefits when equated to search engine optimization, among these is that with PPC advertisements you are able to see an almost instant result, you place an ad. You can be sure that inside minutes you'll begin to appear when individuals search for those keywords, and you'll see prompt traffic. In addition to that PPC (particularly AdWords) helps you to be in utter control of your budget.

AdWords lets you set up both an each day and an each month budget, so that you'll never spend more than you specify. The way that AdWords behaves is like an auction, where you arrange the limit that you're wishing to pay per keyword, and Google plays the auctioneer, if your limit is adequate you'll rank for your top keywords.

In terms of disfavors, among the greatest is cost, nowadays it's really costly to buy ads for competitive keywords and a few competitive keywords might wind up costing upwards of a couple of dollars, or even ten per click, and this may add up quick.

for the sake of this discussion I'll center on AdWords, which is Google's PPC system and is the biggest PPC system presently on the net.

PPC has a few clear benefits when equated to search engine optimization, among these is that with PPC advertisements you are able to see an almost instant result, you place an ad. You can be sure that inside minutes you'll begin to appear when individuals search for those keywords, and you'll see prompt traffic. In addition to that PPC (particularly AdWords) helps you to be in utter control of your budget.

AdWords lets you set up both an each day and an each month budget, so that you'll never spend more than you specify. The way that AdWords behaves is like an auction, where you arrange the limit that you're wishing to pay per keyword, and Google plays the auctioneer, if your limit is adequate you'll rank for your top keywords.

In terms of disfavors, among the greatest is cost, nowadays it's really costly to buy ads for competitive keywords and a few competitive keywords might wind up costing upwards of a couple of dollars, or even ten per click, and this may add up quick.

A different disfavor of PPC is that you'll only get traffic so long as you've room in your budget, when your each day/each month budgets are met you'll no longer come up till the fresh cycle begins. It's likewise crucial to note that you'll only capture traffic as long as you continue paying for ads; pay-per-click does nothing for your natural search rankings and once you quit paying your traffic will return to its former state.

As far as analyzing when and if PPC adds up, I'd suggest that there are a few conditions when I'd advise somebody to utilize this service; the first of these is if you've a brand new web site and you need immediate traffic.

A different case where it might be wise to utilize PPC is if you're able to target long tail keywords. Targeting long tail keywords will provide you the greatest bang for your dollar, but as average search volume is small on long tail keywords, you'd have to target many such keywords and handle these actively.

SEO

Concerning the benefit of utilizing search engine optimization to better your organic search rankings there are a few clear benefits, the most crucial benefit is that you're not paying for each click, and a successful SEO campaign may thus achieve a much lower cost in the long-run.

Additionally much traffic that comes to a web site from natural results is higher quality than pay-per-click traffic (individuals who click an natural result are far more probable to be interested in your product/service as likened to individuals who click PPC ads) you are able to therefore be expected to get a much larger conversion rate from your natural search traffic.

In terms of price, SEO is frequently cheaper than PPC in the long-term, but as an SEO campaign calls for at least six months to demonstrate results, it's frequently tough for many to wrap their brains around this.

A different benefit of SEO is that even following the end of a campaign you'll discover the results of the SEO for a long time, although natural search traffic is likely to decay at about the same pace as it came up. A few of the disfavors of SEO are: you don't see instantaneous results; an SEO campaign calls for at least six months to be successful.

Likewise, SEO (or rather low-cost SEO) calls for the client to be proactive; adding to the development of material (blogs, reports...) and depending upon the person this might or might not work.

It's my sincere notion that anybody who's looking to get the best long-run results ought to focus their efforts on SEO; whereas those who bear short term sites or sites that have to have a strong push at a dedicated date ought to center more on pay-per-click.

Finding Good Long Tail Keywords

If doing your keyword search, there are basically, 2 sorts of keywords that you are able to target. These are short tail keywords and long tail keywords. You may call them blanket keywords or narrow keywords too, but generally you'll only discover the terms "keyword" or "long tail keyword". These 2 words are what I'll utilize throughout this section, merely for clarity.

The Research

Centering on long tail keywords may be a really effective technique, as you'll be targeting less competitory niche markets as opposed to a lot of the highly competitory broad keywords. Something that a lot of pros know and comprehend well, is to utilize long tail keywords that specifically target likely buyers that are late in the purchasing cycle.

You'll commonly discover long tail keywords to be between 3 and 6 words long, but may easily be longer. Let me provide a little illustration of how they work. Say you've a site that's devoted to photographs, that's a really broad keyword, and one that would be hard to rank for. Not stating it's impossible, simply that it would take time and work.

The term "photographs" would be a great example of a market but not a niche. There are millions of results that Google extracted. A lot of the sites have a page rank of 5 and 6. Essentially we have to dive in further to discover niches and sub-niches that aren't as competitory.

To perfect a specific niche, we may try the keyword "outside photographs." Now we're getting warmer as results are lower, with some page rank 5 sites as well as a few lower sites. But this keyword is all the same, more competitory than we may like.

"Outside Alaska wildlife photographs" shows still lower broad match results. This is a better result as we narrowed our focus to a sub-niche. This is merely for demonstration intentions, as this keyword doesn't get any searches. My aim is simply to provide you an illustration of what a long tail keyword is.

This sort of keyword won't bestow you as much traffic, but if you discover enough long tail keywords, they may in reality prove themselves really well. You'll commonly draw in more targeted traffic and they're much easier to rank for than the short tail keywords.

Product critique sites are a really great example of sites that rank well for a lot of different long tail keywords. Even if the site owner doesn't recognize it, he or she will begin ranking for particular product names over time. The reason for this is commonly because the page title will include the product model and description as opposed to just broad words for the product.

A word of care however, when arranging keyword research. If you stumble on an awesome keyword that gets a great amount of searches and isn't too competitory, make certain it isn't a keyword with a trademarked company name in it. This may lead to all sorts of headaches that you would be much better off fending off in the first place.

The company may basically send you a cease and desist letter, as well as making you fork over the domain to them. If you've spent a great amount of time working at your site and adding quality material, it could all fail. Better to avoid this.

Most frequently, marketers utilize long tail keywords in an attempt to corner a smaller than medium market, but still one that holds great potential. A different reason to utilize long tail keywords is that they may be less expensive when using PPC bidding like Google AdWords. Fewer individuals tend to place bids on these keywords, therefore keeping the price from going too high.

Domain Name Selection

If you believe the selection procedure and the name you have picked out for your domain name won't make any difference in the search rankings of your fresh or existing site, think once more.

Nowadays more than ever, all search engines do give a lot of weight to the keywords or phrases that are in your URL. Ask any SEO pro that has been in that business for awhile and they'll tell you that the cautious research and the final choice of the domain name you'll utilize may have a tremendous positive affect in the search results pages from any search engine in existence now.

Your URL

Once you have to register a fresh domain name for an existing web site or a new web site under construction, the beginning thing you have to do is decide if it will be a .com, a .net or a .ca domain name, or any additional variations, as there are many.

If you truly wish to score high and closer to the top in the search engines, then attempt to get a domain name that has 1 or 2 (or 3) of your most crucial keywords in it, as it will greatly help you in the results pages when individuals type in keywords that are intimately affiliated with the theme of your web site. Likewise, for that extra 'punch' in the search engines, I advise that you put a dash in between them, like this: www.your-main-keywords.com

Many major search engines now treat hyphenated domain names as separated words. If these separated words happen to be your most crucial keywords, you're ahead of the game. As a few will tell you that dashes in domain names look clumsy and I fully agree, if you are able to, attempt also registering the

non-hyphenated version also, like :
www.yourmainkeywords.com

If you aren't prepared to construct your site immediately, there are likewise many additional options that may be added to any registered domain name at any time, like the ability to:

• Arrange the domain name on a server with a "Coming Soon" page
• Temporarily re-direct the URL to a different place of your choice
• Temporarily re-direct to a subdirectory of a different URL
• Begin utilizing your new domain name e-mail address (highly suggested)
• Lend relevant body text & keywords to your "Coming Soon" page

There are significant advantages to having your own domain name, like:

1. Branding - Your site address may be a valuable brand name for you. You want individuals to recall it and utilize it on a habitué basis, with every use acting as another brand reinforcement. You lose that solid identity if your visitors have to put something like
www.yourcompany.ispname.othername.com

2. Independence - Should your ISP or hosting service supplier no longer meet your needs or leaves the business , you'll have to move your site's URL and traffic along with the physical shift of your site's server IP address. After all, you've invested time and cash to build up traffic, so you shouldn't have to begin all over again merely because your needs shift or for whatever other reason. In the net world, registered domain names are affiliated with name servers.

When you choose to change the location of your site, your new name servers will be updated in the who-is record held by your registrar. As a result, your site visitors will mechanically be sent to your new host. The bottom line is that you maintain all your traffic and all your sales. If you don't own your domain name, you won't have the luxury of taking your traffic with you.

3. Marketing - Your company or business alone gets to enjoy the increased traffic from each dollar passed marketing your site. If you don't have your own domain name, the company affiliated with your site name will instead glean the benefits of your promotional endeavors.

The cautious selection and wording of your domain name is among the most vital parts of the first steps in setting up any site, old or new. As I've discussed above, it may have a drastic affect in the search engine results pages (SERP's). In a few extreme cases, and depending upon the competitiveness of your industry, it may almost mean the difference between a winner and failure, as far as its visibleness in the search engines is related.

When you have a domain name that was correctly selected, both for your most crucial keywords and perhaps your branding, what's left is the cautious optimization of your web site to ensure all that supplied visibility in the search engines.

Think about a business site just as any other business asset. It's an un-tangible, marketable title of property that may grow substantially in value and it ought to become an crucial ally to your business, while at the same time help you in your long-run promotional efforts.

Choosing The Best Product Title For Your Keyword

Product name keywords are a gravid way to get to the top of Google, and beginning seeing the quickest sales. But, I've heard a lot of individuals saying, "There's too much rivalry in my niche, so the product name keywords are not going to go"

I have to say that what I've seen has been really different. Let's take the health niche, among the most competitive niches on the net.

Your Product Keywords

As I carried out my research, I considered three of the highest gravity merchandise suppliers on Clickbank, and I was amazed to see how little competition there truly was.

Here is where most individuals bomb. They view 1or 2 highly searched keywords such as "Product Name" review and that's it.

Doing a little research, I discovered over twenty keywords across these three highly competitive products in that rigorous niche. Each one of them is highly directed to purchasers, with very little SEO rivalry. The search volumes range anyplace from a hundred monthly searches to five thousand with precise match, and even larger on the liberal match searches.

That's a lot of keywords that you may be targeting that would convert truly well to sales, but most individuals merely are not "wasting their time" on these keywords. I hear individuals telling me that they're too competitive and they can't acquire ranking for them.

I decided to have a look at a few physical products inside the niche. I discovered that this was even easier. I discovered one that the keyword was Buy x product name with over 5,000 precise match monthly searches and not any of the pages on page one had any on page search engine optimization, and they weren't big authority sites. One of the pages had zero links to the page, and less than five hundred to the site, and it was in the top ten.

So, please take a little time to do a little research into the product name keywords, and utilize that research to begin setting link building goals. Then, center your link building efforts on these pages instead of the general content on your site. They'll rank faster, and you'll see higher conversions than you will on general content with an advertisement injected.

How to discover which products in the Clickbank Marketplace are worth marketing via SEO?

Among the greatest affiliate marketing trends of late (and rightfully so as it works) is going to the Clickbank market, browsing through

www.ingramcontent.com/pod-product-compliance
Lightning Source LLC
Chambersburg PA
CBHW071151220526
45468CB00003B/1019